Little Gems
Gervase Phinn

Dalesman

First published in Great Britain 2004
by Dalesman Publishing Company Limited
The Water Mill, Broughton Hall,
Skipton North Yorkshire BD23 3AG
www.dalesman.co.uk

Introductory text and editorial selection
© Gervase Phinn 2004
Poems, stories and illustrations
© the contributors 2004

A British Library Cataloguing-in-Publication record
is available for this book.

ISBN 1 85568 212 5

Designed by Butler & Tanner Ltd
Colour origination by Grasmere Digital Imaging Limited
Printed and bound in Spain

PUBLISHER'S NOTE

The Publishers express its gratitude to the children whose poems,
stories and illustrations are reproduced in this book. Copyright is expressly
reserved on their behalf. However, given the nature of the material, it has not
been possible, despite every effort by Gervase Phinn and Dalesman Publishing
Company, to contact every contributor. In lieu of copyright fees, Dalesman
Publishing Company has made a donation to
the British Dyslexia Assocation.

CONTENTS

Introduction

One delightful and unexpected result of the publication of my autobiographical accounts about my time as school inspector in the Yorkshire Dales is the phenomenal amount of mail I have received. Interested readers have entertained me with letters, cards, anecdotes, poems and little stories about what their children and grandchildren have said. Some were witty, others hilarious and a few were deeply poignant.

Robert Flanagan, director of Dalesman Publishing, suggested that I might like to let others share in my enjoyment of the pieces and further suggested that we ask readers of *Dalesman* magazine to submit their own 'little gems' to add to the collection. Hence this anthology, which I hope you will enjoy reading as much as I have compiling.

I am very grateful for all those who took the time and trouble to send me so much wonderful material. It has not always been possible to trace the author of every piece, so I extend my thanks to all those who contributed anonymously. Sadly, I cannot publish all the 'little gems' because there were so many; I have had to settle for selecting my special favourites.

Acknowledgements

Thanks go to the pupils and staff of the following schools for their help in providing illustrations: Leamington Primary and Nursery School, Sutton-in-Ashfield; All Saints C E Primary School, Aston; Holy Trinity C E (Aided) Primary School, Leeds; Follifoot C E Primary School, Harrogate; Hookstone Chase Primary School, Harrogate; Wilmslow Preparatory School, Cheshire; Christ the King R C Primary School, Thornaby, Stockton-on-Tees; Polam Hall Junior School, Darlington; St Mary Magdelene R C Primary School, Milton Keynes.

The following *Dalesman* readers have kindly contributed to the text: Tony Atkins; E E Avill; Geoff Beecroft; Mr R Billups; Harold Blackburn; Margaret Bottomley; Dorothy Brown; Mrs R E Brown; Don Bullough; Pat Burke; Reginald P Burn; Mrs P Carroll; Betty Charlesworth; Joyce Clarke; Miss E Clarkson; Marilyn Connors; Barbara Cottiswood; Vicky Crossfield; Mrs Dorothy Croxford; Mrs B Cunliffe; Marian Deeds; Ian Denison; Irene Dick; Barbara Dobson; Mrs B Eddon; John Evans; Meg Fellows; Colin Fletcher; Elsie M Fletcher; Mrs Muriel Fryatt; Mrs F M Garth; H Goodall; Anne Gordon; F P Hargreaves; H W Higginbottom; E Holmes;

Glenys Hughes; Jean Hughes; Marcia Hunt; Daphne Ibbott; Mrs J S Ibbotson; Dorothy Jackson; Jane Jackson; Wm A Jagger; Mrs L Johnson; Doris Lomax; Mrs D Lord; Penny Marfleet; John Marsden; Mrs J McCormack; Mrs Irene Meggison; Edith Morgan; Mrs M Muirhead; Harry Myers; Georgina Newton; Gillian Osborn; Brenda Parker; Barbara Payne; Morris Pearson; Mrs M Peason; Bruce Poll; Ernest Pollard; Shirley Ramsey; Nora Riley; Marie Robinson; Hugh Rowland; Mrs C M Sadler; Mrs Marian Samme; Pauline and Geoff Schofield; Mary and Bryan Shackleton; D H Shepherd; Anita Simcox; Mrs P Slater; Mr & Mrs Roy Smart; Moira Smith; R G Smith; Sally Smith; Connie Staples; Joan Stephenson; David Sumner; Elspeth Tanner; Mavis Thomas; Edward Thompson; Mrs D Thompson; Joan Thompson; Mrs M Thompson; Anne Thorpe; Miss Margaret Thorp; Miss A Townson; Mrs J M Waller; Mary Walsh; Yvonne Warburton; Edna Ward; John Ward; Connie Waters; Mrs Janice M Watson; Rosemary Wells; Bernard Wilkinson; Marian Williams; Meg Williams; Betty Wilson; Margaret Wilson; Barbara Winkfield; Neville Withers; Mrs Anne P Wood.

That's no lady, that's my Grandma

Grannies and Grandpas

The relationship between grandparents and their grand-children is rather different from that between parents and their children. Grannies and grandpas, in my experience, tend to be more patient, better listeners, less critical and, dare I say it, more indulgent than their own offspring.

It was the weekly ritual for my mother, well into her eighties, to come around for Sunday lunch. From her vantage point in the most comfortable chair in the corner of the sitting room, she would watch as my wife Christine and I attempted to bring up our four children. One Sunday I had occasion to chastise Matthew, then aged six, for his untidy bedroom. Stabbing the air with a finger, I ordered him: 'Up those stairs now, young man, and tidy your bedroom! Do you follow my drift?' Matthew at first looked suitably contrite but then a small smile appeared on his lips, then a grin to be followed by giggles and finally guffaws. I ballooned with anger. Then I caught sight of my mother in the mirror. She was sitting behind me pulling the most ridiculous faces and wiggling her fingers in front of her nose.

'Mother!' I snapped rather pompously. 'I am trying to instil some discipline here. You are not helping matters!'

'Oh, do be quiet,' she told me. 'You're not talking to teachers now.'

'Mother …!' I began.

'Don't mother me. He's a lovely little boy is Matthew. He's kind, compassionate, gentle and well behaved. You should be telling him that, not hectoring him. Goodness me, there are more important things in life than an untidy room and yours was like a tip when you were a boy.'

Father and son were stuck for words.

She continued. 'I don't suppose I should tell your daddy off in front of you, Matthew,' she said, 'but he's wrong.' Then she gave me a knowing look and one of her smiles, and added 'And he's my little boy'.

Having read this account, you will understand why the poem which begins this section on grannies and grandpas has a particular resonance for me.

My Nan

I like my Nan.
She's round and wrinkly and powdery
And smells of flowers and soap.
She's as comfy as a cushion to sit on.
When my Mum shouts at me
I go to my Nan.
She cuddles me and says,
'Never mind love,
Your Mum was like that
When she was a little girl –
A real grumpybum!'

Mark (aged nine)

At our granddaughter's third birthday party, I was taking photographs when one little boy chimed up: 'Jamie Lee, that lady is taking your picture.'

'That's no lady!' said my granddaughter. 'That's my grandma!'

A week prior to Christmas, I was shopping with my small grandson in a supermarket. As we passed a freezer, I asked him: 'Why do you think that freezer is full of frozen turkeys?'

'To make sure they're dead,' he replied.

Granddaughter asking her rather diminutive grandfather:

'Granddad, why are you so small for your age?'

My Grandma

I loved my Grandma
She was very thoutgull
Her hair was like silver
And her face like gold
Eyes like emerolds

That glinted in the sun.
She was very preicious.

My Grandma

I loved my Grandma.
She was very thoughtful.
Her hair was like silver
And her face like gold,
Eyes like emeralds
That glinted in the sun.
She was very precious.

Amy (aged six)

'Grandpa, were you in the first war?'
'No, I hadn't been born.'
'Were you in the second war?'
'No, I wasn't old enough.'
Short pause for thought.
'Couldn't you go out and start one?'

—

I have seven grandsons. When reaching the age of seven I decide to take each of them to Legoland for the weekend. Michael had been and now it was Glenn's turn. His younger brother, Roger, was upset and wanted to go with him.

'Well, Roger,' I explained, 'in two years time it will be your turn to go and after you there is still Douglas, Cameron, Laurence and Jack.'

'Never mind, Grandma,' consoled Roger, 'I don't expect you will live that long.'

—

Overheard, my small grandchild and her little friend in deep conversation: 'Well, my Daddy says my Grannie's past her sell-by date.'

—

'Grannie,' said Bethany, aged five, 'I know the "F" word.'
'Oh dear!' I said in mock horror, 'you must never say it.'
'I don't, Grannie,' she replied. 'I say trump.'

My Granddad

He is bald my granddad is,
Got no hair at all.
Lots of crinklies round his eyes
And on his cheeks as well.
He laughs at me and Natalie.
His face goes all funny.
Makes wrinkles on his face
Like lots of lines
On my trousers.

Luke (aged six)

Grandson to grandfather: 'Who'll get the fish and chips when you've gone to heaven?'

—

I was at my dressing table, putting some lipstick on and getting ready to go to a WI meeting. My granddaughter, Amy, aged six, was combing my hair.

'Can't find any nits yet, Grannie,' she told me.

Dalesman Grandfather

Old man, smoky beard,
Sunshine smile and haystack hair,
Hands like roots and corn gold skin,
He doesn't have a single care.

Old man, falcon nosed,
Bent old back and raven's eye,
Thin as a scarecrow in his fields,
He stands and sees the world go by.

Daniel (aged ten)

A little Gunnerside tot was looked after by both grans but spent a lot of time with her Dales grannie. On being complimented on her new cardigan by the 'off com'd un' grandmother, little Ruth tugged at the sleeve, grimaced and said, 'Ee, there's no body in this – it won't last five minutes!'

—

Grandson: 'Granddad, we've been asked to take something very very old into school. Will you come in with me tomorrow?'

—

Zachary, my great-nephew, all of seven years old, was upset to hear that his granddad had undergone open heart surgery. On a visit to the hospital he informed his parents seriously that he had decided what he was going to say to his granddad when he saw him: 'Granddad, I love you very much – but with a tinge of sadness.'

My Granny

My Grannie says I am a little chatterbox.
She says I talk ten to the dozen.

Chatter chatter, chatter.
Natter, natter, natter.

My Grandpa says, 'Never mind poppet.
You take after your grannie.

Chatter chatter, chatter.
Natter, natter, natter.

She's the world champion talker.'

Elizabeth (aged six)

I'm eighty-two years old and was having an afternoon snooze on the settee when in comes my granddaughter. 'Wake up, Granddad,' she ordered, 'this is my new friend, Michael. He hasn't got a granddad and I've brought him in to show him what one looks like.'

—

My great-granddaughter, Ruth Hannah, aged five, informed me: 'Gramps, you have got a beard.'
  'No, Ruth, I have a shave every morning.'
  'Yes, you have. It's up your nose.'

Grandpa

My Grandpa is old now.
His head is as bald as a hard-boiled egg
But inside millions of things are going on.

My Grandpa is old now,
But when he sneezes
He blows the leaves off the trees.

My Grandpa is old now,
But when he walks
His legs go snip-snap like a pair of scissors.

My Grandpa is old now,
But when he smiles
The sun comes out and the birds sing.

My Grandpa is old now.
But he doesn't act his age.

Elizabeth (aged seven)

I explained to my grandson, aged five, who had asked where my dog was, that Rusty was very old and tired and had had a long and happy life and that the vet had 'put him to sleep.'

'When will you be going to the vet then, Grandma?' he asked.

—

At lunch, my small grandson asked casually: 'Granddad, can I have this house when you pop your clogs?'

—

Whilst recovering from a cataract operation I asked my granddaughter to pick up her toys, explaining that I couldn't bend down yet. 'Why? Will your eye fall out, Gran?' she asked.

—

I am a very careful driver, if a little on the slow side. I was taking my small grandson, Harry, aged six, to a birthday party and we were running rather late. As I trundled along the road, he gave a great heaving sigh and said in a very exasperated tone of voice: 'Step on it Gran, for God's sake. We'll be here all day at this rate.'

On another occasion I nearly crashed the car because of my uncontrollable laughter. Harry, strapped in the back, watched fascinated as an impatient young driver overtaking me after a road junction, made a very rude sign in my direction.

'Grannie,' Harry said cheerfully, 'I think the man in the car in front is showing you his poorly finger.'

—

Hayley, my three-year-old granddaughter, came into the bathroom just in time to see me remove my false teeth.

'Jeremy! Jeremy!' she screamed to her brother. 'Come quickly, Nana is doing magic!'

—

Four-year-old granddaughter staring intently at her granddad's bald pate: 'Granddad, you haven't been eating your crusts.'

—

When I was honorary curator of the Manor House Museum, Ilkley, I encouraged children to bring finds, always hoping something of importance would turn up. In came a little girl with three stones in her hand.

'What are these, dear?' I asked.

'My granny's gallstones,' was the smiling reply.

———

My granddaughter, Sydney, when she was four, decided to comb everyone's hair. When she got to me, she ran the comb gently up and down and then stopped, sat back and remarked: 'Papa, you might have lots of wrinkles but you have the most handsome hair.'

———

Grandson was visiting grandma for the day. Grandma said: 'You have got a bad cough.'

His reply was: 'I've got one at home as well.'

———

Granddad, collecting his small granddaughter from school, asked her to take her school bag and coat out to the car. 'You're not too old to carry things yourself, granddad, you know,' she replied pertly.

———

A niece, now in her sixties, had a grandfather who had very large ears. One day she said to her mother, 'When Grandpa dies will he become an angel?'

The mother replied, 'I expect so, dear, why do you ask?'

'Oh, I thought he'd become an elf,' replied the child.

———

My granddaughter, aged six, came into the bathroom where I was quietly removing, with the aid of tweezers, an odd whisker on my chin.

'Grandma,' she said, 'I will be glad when I am old and have hairs on my face.'

—

Felicity, aged three, asked me why she hadn't got a granddad. I explained to her that he had gone to Heaven.

'I suppose you'll be next,' said Felicity in a matter-of-fact little voice.

'There is great-grandma,' I reminded her.

'Yes, but she doesn't go anywhere by herself,' replied the child.

—

My granddaughter Jessica was watching in fascination as I cleaned my false teeth in the bathroom. I explained that, unlike hers, mine weren't real and I take them out to wash them to keep them nice and fresh. She noticed a bar of Pears soap on the washbasin – the round, brown, transparent kind. 'Is that your tongue, Grannie?' she asked.

Mummy, what does God stand on?

God, religion and going to church

When it comes to God and religion, young children are immensely disarming, and their questions and observations frequently leave the adult lost for words.

On a visit to a school deep in the Yorkshire Dales, I observed the school assembly taken by a very genial vicar. He started his assembly by asking the children to try and guess what was in his head. He told them that, as he had walked through the churchyard on his way to the school that morning, he had seen something behind a tree. It had been grey and hairy with a great bushy tail and little darting, black, shiny eyes like beads.

'And what do you think I'm talking about?' he had asked the children.

A large, ruddy-complexioned boy with a mop of very fair hair replied: 'I know it's Jesus, vicar, but it sounds like a squirrel to me.'

On another occasion, a young and very enthusiastic curate read, from a large crimson-covered children's Bible, the parable of 'The Good Samaritan' and explained to his young audience how the story taught us all how to lead better lives. He could see by the fidgeting and turning of heads that it was not having a massive impact, so he decided to finish. But not before posing one final question.

'And what would you say to Jesus,' he asked, holding high the red book like some preacher of old, 'if He were to walk into the hall this morning?'

The boy on the front row thought for a moment, then raised his hand and said loudly, 'I'd give 'im that there book, vicar, and I'd say, "Jesus Christ – this is your life".'

I fared little better in an assembly that I took. I related the parable on 'The Lost Sheep' and asked the children the question: 'Why do you think the shepherd risked losing all his other sheep just for the one which was lost?', and some bright spark replied, ''Appen it were t' tup.'

Many of the 'little gems' in this section bring a smile to the lips, but the first poem I find extremely affecting coming, as it does, from one so young.

God

When I was little,
I thought that God
Was like Captain Birdseye
Without the fish fingers.
I thought that God
Always smiled and had a friendly face,
That he was tall and kind
And never shouted.
Now I am older,
I think that God
Is like an old old man
Without any children.
I think that God
Has a sad and tired face,
That he cries
And groans
To see the world
He made.

Sean (aged nine)

Child to vicar: 'Are you growing a beard to be more like Jesus?'

—

The first time our son Ian was shown the vicarage, he asked: 'Is that where they make Vick?'

God.

When I was little,
I thought that God
Was like Captain Birdseye
Without the fishfingers.
I thought that God
Always smiled and had a friendly face,
That he was tall and kind
And never ever shouted.

Now I am older,
I think that God
Is like an old old man
Without any children.
I think that God
Has a sad and tired face,
That he cries
And groans
To see the world
He made.

Lucy's Carol

When the Baby borned
Joseph said to Mary,
'What am I going to do about
This little-born Jesus Baby Christ?
I never knew it was going to be like this,
With all these angels and kings
And shepherds and stars and things;
It's got me worried, I can tell you,
On Christmas Day in the morning.'
Mary said to Joseph,
'Not to worry darling,
Dear old darling Joseph;
Everything's going to be all right,
Because the Angel told me not to fear;
So just hold up the lamp,
So I can see the dear funny sweet little face
Of my darling Little-born Jesus Baby Christ'.
Joseph said to Mary,
'Behold the handy-man of the Lord.'
Happy Christmas, happy Christmas'
Christ is born today.

Lucy (aged four,
recorded by her mother as she talked to her dolls)

At the Christmas morning service, the last carol had been sung and there was a moment's quiet before 'the dismissal'. In the silence as we all bowed our heads in prayer, an impatient little voice echoed around the church: 'Can we go now, mummy?'

The reply from the priest was instantaneous: 'In a minute.'

—

The vicar asked the children: 'Now, what do you know about Jesus?'

My son, Joshua, aged six, replied: 'Well, I know he likes fish.'

—

On a dark, clear, starry night, grandpa took his four-year-old granddaughter into the garden for a lesson on the 'Sky at Night'.

'What do they call it up there?' she asked, staring upwards.

'That's Heaven,' explained grandpa. 'It's where all the good people go.'

'Well, if I don't like it the first time I go,' the little girl told him, 'I won't go again.'

—

Christopher, aged five, looking into the sky: 'Mummy, what does God stand on? Perhaps it's a hard cloud.'

—

A mother was teaching her little girl the Lord's Prayer, asking the child to repeat each phrase after her. One evening the little girl announced proudly that she could say it all by herself and began with great gusto. She recited the prayer perfectly until she came to the line: 'And deliver us from evil.' Instead she said proudly: 'And deliver us some e-mail.'

—

Emily, aged three, asked: 'Mummy, does Jesus tell us everything?'

'Yes,' replied her mother.

'Well, I think he's telling us to go to Toys R Us', said the child.

—

My son, in primary school, spent much time drawing. His teacher asked him about one particular sketch.

'Who is this?' she enquired.

'God,' he replied,

'No-one knows what God looks like,' she informed him.

'Well they will when they see this,' replied the child.

—

When the vicar entered the classroom, one small boy sighed 'Oh God' under his breath.

Without pausing for thought, the vicar smiled and said loudly, 'No, not God, just one of His friends.'

—

The bishop had visited my grandson's infant school, and let the children try on some of his regalia and hold his precious crosier. Following his visit, the children were asked to write and thank him. Joshua wrote: 'Thank you for coming into our school, Bishop John. I now know what a crook looks like.'

—

When my godson Oliver was asked what he would like to give up for Lent, he replied: 'School.'

—

Small child in church during an inordinately long sermon: 'Grannie, is it still Sunday?'

—

A small girl who was making her first Holy Communion seemed to be rather nervous and insisted on returning to the toilet in the church. Annie, my wife, of course allowed her to go again but did say she should have gone before coming into church. When the child appeared after her second visit she announced:

'Hasn't God got a lovely toilet?'

—

I was telling my small granddaughter about the journey of the Israelites into the wilderness and the miraculous provision of manna. On finishing the story I asked the little one what she thought manna was.

'Well, Grandpa,' she said confidently, 'you see there are good mannas and bad mannas.'

—

The vicar was addressing the infant school assembly. 'When I last saw some of you children,' he said, 'you were brought into my church as babies, all in white with your mummies and daddies, family and friends. It was a very very special occasion. Does anyone know what I did to you when you were a tiny baby and were brought to church?' The children stared wide-eyed but silent. 'Well, I will give you a clue,' continued the vicar, undeterred by the lack of response. 'The word I am thinking of begins with a curly C.' He stared at the blank faces and persevered. 'I chr …chr…chr …anyone know?'

A child shouted out: 'Crucified.'

—

At Sunday morning service, the vicar referred to a verse from the Bible: 'He that hath ears to hear, let him hear.' He then asked the children: 'And what do you do with your ears?'

In a flash a little lad raised his hand and called out: 'You wash behind them.'

———

The preacher entered the pulpit and the small door closed behind him. He proved to be rather flamboyant, waving his arms about in dramatic gestures to emphasise a point. A clear penetrating little voice of the small child echoed around the church: 'Granny, whatever will he do if he gets out?'

———

My brother John, a Roman Catholic priest, had all the small children around the altar at Mass. 'God loves us all and takes care of us,' he told the little ones. 'He's a very good listener too, so when we want to thank Him or ask Him for His help, He listens. Now children, how do we talk to God?' he asked, expecting them to respond by saying that we all say our prayers every night. He was surprised and not a little amused when one bright spark shouted: 'You could always text Him.'

———

At the rear of our church is a set of boxes and on each is a label: 'For the altar flowers', 'For the candles', 'For the missions'. My little grandson Jamie, aged six, was very keen to show me how good a reader he was and recited every label with ease. He paused at the last box and thought for moment. 'This one's useful, Granddad,' he said, 'if your tummy's feeling a bit poorly.' On the front of the box was written: 'For the sick.'

———

When the local parish priest visited our first school, one child asked him: 'Why do they call you father if you haven't any children?'

—

My little granddaughter Katherine told me she was about to make her 'First Holy Communication'.

—

My thirteen-year-old stepson was playing football with some friends in a local park when he was approached by a pair of missionaries from the evangelical church.

'What would you do if we told you that Jesus saves?' they asked.

The youngster replied: 'I'd put him in goal.'

—

At Sunday school, the young vicar asked the children what Jesus did first thing in the morning and last thing at night, something that we too should do. He, of course, was expecting: 'Say our prayers'. The reply from one little boy was: 'Go to the toilet.'

—

Young child just before we said our prayers: 'I'm sick of talking to God with my eyes closed.'

Mummy, I know a dirty word

The things children say

Smile and the young child will smile back. Little ones don't know what cynicism is; they don't know how to curl a lip and are unconcerned about skin colour, background, race, religion, accent and the things which often cause so much distress and conflict in the world.

Little children have no conception of status or rank, and judge those they meet without preconceptions. They are innately curious, open, innocent, spontaneous and honest. Sometimes, it has to be said, they are a little too honest.

Once on a school visit in York I was informed by a six-year-old child: 'Have you ever thought that when I'm twenty-one, you'll probably be dead?' On another occasion, I commented to a little boy in the infant classroom that his writing at the top of the page was lovely and neat, but went all squiggly at the bottom. 'I know,' he said sighing, 'this pen's got a life of its own.'

On a visit to a Rotherham school with the mayor to see the Christmas play, we were puzzled to notice that all the children were coming out of the building and heading for home.

'Where's everyone going?' his worshipful asked a little boy with hair like a lavatory brush and a face as speckled as hen's egg. 'We've come for the nativity.'

'Aaah, well, it's off,' the little boy informed him.

'Off?' repeated the mayor.

'Aye,' said the child. 'T' Virgin Mary's got nits.'

I recall the time during my first year as an inspector when I found a corner of an infant classroom set out as a baby clinic and a small girl clutching a large doll to her chest. She was surrounded by scales, towels, feeding bottles, a plastic bath and a toy cot.

As I approached, she looked up alarmed. 'Go away!' she cried. 'I'm breast feeding.'

So, 'Here's to the child and all he or she has to teach us', as the old Irish saying tells us. Enjoy the bluntness and honesty of the children in this section; the things they say in the small anecdotes, cameos, poems and prose pieces are guaranteed to delight.

The Owl

The bird I am going to tell you about is the owl. The owl cannot see by day and at night is as blind as a bat. I do not know anything else about an owl so I will tell you about a cow.

The cow is a mammal. It has six sides – a right, left, upper and below. At the back it has a tail on which hangs a brush. With this it sends the flies away so that they do not fall into its milk.

The head of the cow is for the purpose of growing horns on and so that the mouth can be somewhere. The horns are to butt with and the mouth is to moo with.

The legs of the cow go right down to the ground.

Under the cow hangs the milk. It has been arranged for milking. When people milk, the milk comes out and there's never an end to the supply. How the cow does this I do not know but it makes more and more. The cow has a fine sense of smell. You can smell it far away. This is the reason for the fresh air in the countryside.

The man cow is called an ox. It is not a mammal.

The cow does not eat much but what it eats it eats twice so that it always gets enough. When the cow is hungry it moos and when it says nothing it is because its insides are full of grass.

Martha (aged six)

Paul, aged three, whispered: 'Mummy, I know a dirty word.'

'Do you, Paul?' asked his shocked mother.

'Dustbin,' confided the child.

—

Paige and Jay, aged six and four respectively, were in trouble because someone had bitten a piece out of the bath sponge. Paige pleaded her innocence: 'It wasn't me honestly and that's the truth', she said.

Jay looked up at his daddy with eyes as big and as round as saucers, and said: 'It wasn't me and I am making the truth up.'

———

Miriam, aged six, on being told sadly by her mother that daddy wouldn't be able to go on holiday with them one year because he was so busy, shrugged and replied: 'I can live with that'.

———

I tried to be as sensitive and tactful as possible when my small granddaughter, Lucy, asked where my dog was. 'It was time for him to go,' I explained in a very sad and quiet voice, 'and the vet had to put him to sleep.'

'You mean he killed him,' Lucy told me.

———

Following a little accident on the hall floor during assembly, an infant explained to his teacher: 'My willy went out of control.'

———

I overheard a conversation in my local market town between two five-year-old girls:

'Sylvia, have you got that chewing-gum I lent you?'

'No, I've lost it.'

'Well, you'll have to find it, 'cos it's our Robert's.'

———

Andrew, aged four, came dashing into the house shouting: 'Mummy, Mummy, my caterpillars in the jar on the windowsill are turning into Christians.'

———

I took my five-year-old daughter to London Zoo, and we were standing in a crowd watching the chimpanzees. A very obviously male chimpanzee was lying on his back lifting a baby chimp up and down.

My daughter said, 'Oh, look at that mummy chimpanzee playing with her baby.'

Without thinking I said, 'That's not a mummy, it's a daddy.'

Quick as a flash my daughter said, 'Oh, of course it's a daddy. It's just lying around doing nothing.'

———

Four-year-old asking his father: 'Dad, you know that you said that you would never get this model railway finished? Well, the day you die, will you write down all that still needs doing and I'll finish it?'

———

My daughter, aged six, flung her arms around me, buried her nose in my tummy, breathed deeply and exclaimed, 'Oh, I do like the smell of old age.'

———

Sarah found a dead mouse. We buried it and told her that it had gone to Heaven. After a while she came to me and said: 'Grandma, shall we dig it up and see if it's gone yet?'

———

Dear Mr. Phinn,

Please (pretty please) can you come to ossially open Hade Edge School. Your book "Royster Knapper" is brilliant! Well so I've heard.

After you open our school, you can join in with our party! I dont whats happening about our party, because its teachers biusness.

And after that, you can have a walk arouned Holmesties, our reservoir. Smell the fresh air!

So please come here. You need to! Everyone else couldnt come so you should!

The Invitation

Dear Mr Phinn,

   Please (pretty please!) can you come to officially open Hade Edge School?

   Your book 'Royston Knapper' is brilliant! Well so I've heard. After you open our school, you can join in with our party. I don't know what's happening about our party, because it's teachers' business. And after that you can have a walk around Holmesties, our reservoir. Smell the fresh air.

   So please come here. You need to! Everyone else couldn't come so you should!

Sam Walls (aged eleven)

A Roman Soldier Writes Home

Greetings Paulinus,

   It's been a bad week!

I've just got back from boring old Britain. It's cold and gloomy, wet and windy. And you should see the Britons. Ugh! Big, ugly, smelly, fat, screaming, hairy yobs.

   The surroundings are horrible and Sergeant Andus is nasty to us all. I miss the sunshine and the grapes and the wine.

   I will have to stop now as my spaghetti is getting cold.

Dominicus

PS   I also have diarrhoea.

Dominic (aged nine)

When I was four, I was taken out to tea for the first time. A plate of exceedingly tiny sandwiches was offered to mother, with the suggestion that she should take two while the plate was there. She duly did. Then it came to my turn so I said, 'I'll take two, while I'm here, shall I?'

—

A small boy was invited out to tea by a certain Miss Somebody in the locality. During tea he suddenly addressed his hostess, saying: 'Are you called Miss because you have missed being married?'

—

My son, aged two, is beginning to talk. The other day he pointed to the half-moon and commented: 'Sunshine broken.'

Becky

Becky didn't like reading,
She didn't like singing,
She didn't like riding her bike,
She didn't like running,
She didn't like shopping,
She didn't like watching TV,
She didn't like sweets.
She was a pain in the Bum.

Laura (aged six)

Becky dident
like reading
she dident
like singing
she dident
like riding
her bike
She dident
like runing
She dident
like shoping

she dident
like waching
TV
she dident
like sweets
She was a
pain in the
Bum

One foggy day, our small grandson, after looking pensively out of the window for some time, asked: 'Gran, where's the outside gone?'

—

I asked my infant daughter if she would like an ice cream (her very first). She watched several children eating ice cream cornets, and replied: 'Yes please, Daddy, I'll have one with a handle on.'

Lost

One day my mummy and daddy went to Ripon and I went too. Daddy went in a bookshop with the brothers and mummy went in a dress shop with me. I hid in some coats. They could not find me. mummy cried and daddy panicked. The brothers stood as still as stone. After a few minutes I popped out my head and said: 'Peepo.'

'You little horror,' said mummy.

Elizabeth (aged seven)

My young daughter, when we were visiting another family, was on her very best behaviour during the main course. As we continued to chat and no move was made to bring dessert, she asked politely: 'Would you like me to have some pudding?'

—

It was a particularly appetising school dinner, but no second helpings were available. A young 'hopeful', receiving this news, sadly remarked: ' If there's ivver owt good, there's nivver nowt left.'

—

Mark, as a very young child, eyed some vegetables on his plate with grave suspicion and asked his mother what they were. She explained that they were called parsnips. He nodded. 'Is that what they sing about at Christmas time?' he asked. We looked puzzled so he explained: 'Parsnips in a pear tree?'

—

Our two-year-old daughter, in the middle of potty training, announced she wanted to go to the toilet at a very inconvenient time. Her grandma told her to wait and try to hold it. Her immediate response was: 'Nanna, I can't hold it because it hasn't got a handle.'

—

After watching my four-year-old niece drawing pictures of people with purple hair and in garish garb, using felt tip pens with reckless abandon, I became worried that she may be colour blind. Out one day on a walk, I put my fears to the test.

I said, 'If you stood in this field of rape in your yellow play-suit and if I stood by this hawthorn hedge in my dark green tweeds, noone would ever see us, would they?' She rolled her eyes upwards and said pityingly: 'Auntie, I think the word you are seeking is camouflage.'

—

Driving past a gentlemen's toilet, Jamie remarked: 'Auntie, that's where dogs come from.' Puzzled, I asked him why he thought so and he replied: 'Because every time my daddy goes in there, he says he's going to see a man about a dog.'

—

We live near a large lake and many of the frogs, on their travels along the village road, perish beneath the wheels of the traffic. Angus, aged four, looked in amazement at the many bodies which littered the road and asked, 'Auntie, why didn't they look left and right before crossing?'

—

This is a definition of a hill from my mother's remembrance of her schooldays in Bradford, seventy years ago: 'A gret lump o' muck, slantin' up straight.'

—

I am a teacher. One day shopping with my three year old, she asked, 'Mummy, can I have an ice cream, please?'

'No.'

'Well, can I have some sweeties?'

'No.'

'Well, can I have I have a biscuit?'

'No.'

'Well, I don't want another bloody book.'

—

In the 1940s, when I taught at Stetford Junior Commercial School, the entrance examination required students to put words into sentences to show their meanings. One word was 'flourish'. A bright spark wrote: 'Don't forget to flourish the toilet when you've been.'

—

My husband and I and our three sons, Jacob, Thomas and Andrew, aged twelve, nine and six, spent a weekend at a rather exclusive Scottish hotel on special offer. Children under the age of eleven went half price and my husband, being a canny

Yorkshireman, was intent on spending as little money as possible. At the reception desk the young woman asked how many of the children were under eleven.

'All of them,' my husband told her confidently.

'No, Daddy,' piped up Andrew, 'Jacob is twelve.'

'No, I'm not,' snapped his eldest brother, fully aware of his father's reasons for telling the fib and happy to collude.

'Yes, you are,' persisted Andrew, 'and stop kicking me.'

'Ah yes,' said my husband, looking decidedly embarrassed. 'He's just had his birthday.'

'No, he hasn't, Daddy,' exclaimed Andrew, 'his birthday was a long time ago. It was on May 4th.'

'Of course,' mumbled my husband. 'Silly me.' Then he smiled weakly at the very amused receptionist. 'Two children under eleven and one over,' he said sheepishly.

Later in the restaurant I reminded him of the words of Scotland's most famous poet:

'Oh what a tangled web we weave

When first we practise to deceive.'

I know the difference between girls and boys

The facts of life

How many parents have been asked that tricky question: 'Where do I come from?' Children are naturally inquisitive and very persistent when they think they are being fobbed off, given a lame excuse or told a fanciful story.

When my son Dominic was six, he asked the dreaded question: 'Daddy, where do I come from?'

'I'll get your mother,' I said quickly.

The three of us sat him down on the settee, Dominic sandwiched between my wife and me, and tried to explain to him, slowly and honestly, how he came into the world. We told him that daddy loved mummy, and mummy loved daddy, and how sometimes they had an extra-close cuddle. I could hear myself sounding more and more like Joyce Grenfell. I told him about mummy having an egg and daddy having a sperm, and the other facts of life.

'So does that explain it, Dominic?' I asked.

He stared up at me with wide unblinking eyes and sighed heavily. 'No, it doesn't,' he said. 'I just wanted to know where I come from. Andrew comes from Sheffield.'

I was once approached by a small boy in an infant school who announced bluntly: 'I know how to mek babies, you know.'

I smiled, nodded sagely, tried not to look in the least shocked and replied in a very casual voice, 'Really?'

'Aye, I do. I've just learnt how to mek babies.' There was a pregnant pause. 'Do you know how to mek babies then?' he asked.

'I do, yes,' I replied

There was another long pause. 'How do you mek babies, then?' the boy asked, looking me straight in the eye.

'You go first,' I told him.

'Well', he said, 'I knock the "y" off and add "i-e-s".'

My mother was looking after her little cousins, a boy and a girl, who were playing doctors and nurses. After a quiet period the little boy rushed into the room shouting: 'Doctor, doctor, come quick. A baby's been born and we can't find the mother.'

—

My son, aged four, on seeing my bra hanging over a chair back in the bedroom, asked: 'Is that where you keep baby's dinner, Mummy?'

—

My grandson, Callum, aged six, told me, nodding confidently and pointing downwards, 'I know the difference between girls and boys, Grannie.'

'Really,' I replied, imagining the tricky conversation which would ensue.

'It's down there, Grannie.'

'Is it?'

'Boys have bigger feet.'

—

My grandson Christopher and I were playing cricket in the back garden and it was his turn to bowl. Before he did so, he gave me the benefit of his considerable experience (he was six): 'Be very careful, Grandpa, don't let the ball hit you in the nuts. It can be very painful.'

—

I took my little grandson George, aged six, to the swimming baths. As I changed into my trunks, he pointed to a private part of my anatomy and observed: 'I've got one of those, Grandpa.'

'Yes, I know,' I said, 'all little boys have one.'

'My Daddy's got one as well.'

'Yes, I know, and all men have them too.'

'Yours is a lot bigger than mine.'

'Yours will get bigger when you get older,' I told him.

He wrinkled his little nose.

'You're older than Daddy, Grandpa, aren't you?' said George.

'That's right,' I replied.

'Well, why is Daddy's a lot bigger than yours?'

I was stumped.

—

A Yorkshire farmer's wife, mother of six-year-old boy twins, gave birth to another son. The twins were invited to inspect. After a long silence the mother said: 'Have yer got nowt to say to yer new brother?'

'Aye,' one child replied, 'wheerst t' other?'

Once Upon a Time

Once upon a time there was a prince and a princess and they were friends and they played games together and they had fun. Then they had a wedding and after the wedding they went home and then they had some lunch and they had a drink and then they had some pudding. Then they did some palace work.

Then they watched a bit of TV and then they had a bit of tea and a drink and then they had some pudding. Then they went to bed. The next day they had a bit of breakfast and then they had a biscuit and then they had a drink and then they had some pudding. Then they went downstairs and then they got dressed and then they went to hospital and then they had a baby. Then they went home and they had a bit of tea and then they had some pudding.

Jennifer and Claire

My grandson started school in September. After his first week, he came home to say that the teacher had told them that there were three brothers in the class with the same birthday and that they were called 'twiglets'.

—

John, aged three and born a bred on a Dales farm, went to see his mother in hospital to view his new baby brother. He was less interested in the new addition to his family but was fascinated by a black woman in the next bed with her little baby.

'Don't stare,' said John's mum to her little boy, 'it's very rude.'

The black woman smiled and waved, then got out of bed to take the baby for his feed. She put on a white dressing gown and white socks. As she was heading for the door little John, pointing at her, announced: 'Swaledale.'

That's the Head Mystery's room

School and schooldays

Teachers take on the most important role in society: the education of the young. Teaching is demanding, challenging and sometimes frustrating, but there are few jobs which are as exciting and fulfilling. Those who take on this most important role must, of course, be prepared to meet little philosophers and sharp critics, the curious, the precocious, the unpredictable, the charming and, sometimes, the exasperating.

A fellow school inspector was visiting the infant classroom and engaged a little boy in a conversation about dinosaurs.

'You know a lot about these creatures,' he said.

'I know.' The little boy looked up. 'I luv 'em. They're great. I draw 'em all t' time.'

'And are there any around today?'

'Cooarse not. They're all deead. They're hextinct.'

'What does that mean?'

'Deead. Wiped aaht.'

'And why do you think that is?' the inspector asked.

The little boy had thought for a moment. 'Well, mester,' he said, 'that's one of life's gret mysteries, in't it?'

I was once told by a little girl that her auntie had got sixty-five roses.

'Sixty-five roses?' I said. 'She's very lucky your auntie, isn't she?'

The child shook her head. 'No, she's not. It's not nice having sixty-five roses.'

'I thought your auntie would really like so many beautiful coloured flowers with their lovely smell.'

'It's not nice having sixty-five roses.' she persisted quietly.

And then it dawned upon me. Her auntie had just died. These were the flowers at her funeral.

'Has your auntie died?' I asked gently.

'No,' said the child in a voice deep with indignation. 'She's got sixty-five roses.' The teacher, hearing the exchange, and seeing my puzzlement and the child's, explained with a wry smile, 'She means cystic fibrosis, Mr Phinn.'

Teachers

Teachers shout and bawl at us
Making such a massive fuss.
Homework comes in piles and piles,
Essays last for miles and miles.
They give us sums we cannot do
And never think of something new.
Same boring lessons every week
Sending children off to sleep,
Same droning voices every day
How I wish they'd go away.

Andrew (aged nine)

'And when Chicken Licken arrived at the palace, children,' the infant teacher informed her little charges, 'and told the king that the sky was falling down, what do you think the king said?'

'Bloody hell, a talking chicken', replied an infant.

—

Jennie, my daughter, when five, came home and said she had to take something old to school.

'You can take me,' I told her.

'Oh no,' she exclaimed. 'It has to be something precious.'

—

My grandson's school was undergoing a school inspection. I asked Jordan how things were going. 'We're being infected, Grannie,' he told me, 'and I don't like it.'

On Monday Mr Dobson came
into school He was fat
with wiskers and a flat
cap. He woulddent stop
talking. He got boring and
we fell asleep. Mrs Wilson
Said he liked the sound
of his own voice.

The School Inspector Calls

On Monday Mr Dobson came into school. He was fat with whiskers and a flat cap. He wouldn't stop talking. He got boring and we fell asleep. Mrs Wilson said he liked the sound of his own voice.

Amy (aged six)

I taught in an inner-city infant school. Many of the children, although from poor and often difficult backgrounds, were warm and loving. I was reading the story of 'The Three Little Pigs', and told my little charges how the Big Bad Wolf was intent on blowing down the house of straw and gobbling up the first little pig. 'The bastard!' came a small voice from the back.

—

I help voluntarily at a junior and infant school. One of the teachers mentioned to the children that it was my seventieth birthday. A little one piped up: 'Ah, Mrs Thompson, aren't you glad that you are still alive?'

—

Our young daughter Carmel, coming home, was asked by my wife what had happened at school that day. She answered: 'Oh, we have a new headmonster.'

Visit to the Farm

Last Tuesday we went to Wilson's Farm. My friend Mark was sick on the bus – all over the seat, his shoes, his coat and Mrs Thompson. She went mad and smelt horrible. Mark had to put his head in a big blue plastic bucket. Mrs Thompson pulled faces all the way. When we got to the farm, Mark trod in some cow pats.

Mr Wilson, the farmer, said, 'Pooh! Something smells worse than my pigs.'

Mrs Thompson went bright red. Farmer Wilson showed us some horses and pigs and big cows and hens and geese. Then he pointed to a field. 'Look at those heifers,' but I couldn't see any.

Geoffrey (aged six)

Child showing round a new boy: 'That's the Head Mystery's room.'

—

Two infant children in Leeds caught sight of a squirrel outside the classroom window.

'Quick, tell Miss,' cried one.

'Shut yer gob, Gavin,' replied the other. 'She'll 'ave us write abaat the bugger.'

My School

My school is horrid. They give you rotten milk and I can tell you how rotten the milk is. In Class 1, I could not drink all my milk, 'cos it is so rotten so I decided to make a plan.

My teacher was away and the class was took over by Miss Martin and I could not drink it fast because it was so rotten and when the class went out to play, I emptied my milk into the sink and went out to play and Jimmy Bennet was surprised to see

me at play but I didn't mind 'cos God had made me very glad but now I'm in Class Two. I've got good at drinking milk but there was another problem –

Sums. So I got another plan in my head and do you know what it was? It was to cheat. I counted in ones by putting ones all the way up my book until I had sixteen. And that was what the number was at the top of my page so that was another problem dealt with but there was another problem what no one could get rid of but I could and that was writing. So I got near a boy with chicken pox so I could not go to school.

Geoffrey (aged seven)

When I was headteacher of an infant school some years ago, I was telling a small child off for some misdemeanor. He had been throwing stones at other children. He tried to extricate himself from his difficult situation without success and was clearly losing the argument. Then he played his trump card. Wiping away his tears, he took a deep breath and told me pathetically: 'And I'm from a one-parent family, you know.'

—

My grandson Richard, when he was six, wrote in his school journal; 'Last night my daddy beat my mummy again.' He was, as his mother explained to the concerned teacher, referring to Scrabble.

—

The school inspector sat with the infants at lunch. The pudding was a particularly hard and brittle piece of biscuit, and when he tried to stab it with his spoon, it jumped up and out of the bowl. 'Tha wants to put some custard on it, mester,' advised the small boy sitting opposite, 'to stop it leeapin' abaat.'

To Granny and family
Love from Sarah

friendes

Granny

Linda

Samantha

Rory

Sofe

And the greatest of these is love

Children are powerfully affected by those around them. Well before they can speak, they are able understand so much – a smile, a gentle touch, the tone of our voice, a frown. Their great desire in life, as it is for all of us, is to be loved.

When my eldest son Richard graduated from Durham University, the chancellor, Sir Peter Ustinov, draped in his gold-trimmed academic gown and sporting a very impressive mortar board, was interrupted in his address by the loud and happy gurgling of a baby at the rear of the hall. The great man deviated from his speech, and told the young graduands that all that small innocent desired was to be fed, kept warm and to be loved and then he or she would be happy indeed. Perhaps it was a lesson for us all, he told us. The baby babbled on and the chancellor with a wonderfully serious countenance gurgled back, much to everyone's amusement. 'The child has just informed me,' he announced, 'that he is ready to be changed.'

My Sister

My little sister died last night
In the Hospital.
She was four days old.
Only four days old.
And when I saw her for the first time
I don't think I'd ever been as happy.
She was small and crinkled
With big eyes and soft, soft skin
And a smile like a rainbow.
Her fingers were like tiny sticks
And her nails were like little sea shells
And her hair like white feathers.
Now she's gone, and my mum can't stop crying,
And my dad stairs at nothing.
I loved our baby.
I'll never forget her.

James (aged ten)

My Sister.

My little sister died last night
In the Hospital.
She was four days old.
Only four days old.
And when I saw her for the first time.
I do'nt think I'd ever been as happy.
She was so small and crinkled.
With big eyes and soft soft skin.
And a smile like a rainbow.
Her fingers were like tiny sticks.
And her nails like little sea shells.
And her hair like white feathers.
Now shes gone, and my mum can't stop crying,
And my dad stairs at nothing.
I loved our baby.
I'll never forget her.

I married my lass fifty-four years ago after leaving the Scots Guards and recently lost her. I find life without her tough. One day I was feeling very down, when my grandchildren held my hands and said: 'Grandpa, we love you' — a simple expression which made an old soldier feel so much better.

—

I was shopping in Leeds with my four-year-old daughter, and in a large department store she noticed a black woman, the first she had ever seen, and was greatly interested in her. 'Mummy, Mummy, just look at that lady,' she cried, pointing. I was deeply embarrassed and dreaded a further comment. My daughter then added. 'Isn't she beautiful?' If only everybody could see the world through the eyes of a child.

—

'You know, Gran,' Amy, my six-year-old graddaughter told me when I kissed her goodnight, 'I've been thinking. If people minded their own business and loved people, there wouldn't be all this fighting in the world.'

—

'Grannie, I know what people do when they really love each other,' said Roisin, my granddaughter of six. 'I've seen it on the television.'

'Do you dear?', I said, bracing myself for a lesson in the facts of life.

Roisin nodded sagely. 'They hold each other's hands and smile.'

A Child's Prayer

Will you hug me Mummy?
Will you wrap me in your arms
And press your face to mine
And whisper happy memories in my ear.
For when shadows dance around me
And I feel alone in the dark,
I need to recall your gentle touch
And know that you are near.
Will you hold me Daddy?
Will you take my hand
And weave strong fingers into mine,
And tell me how you love me.
For when monsters invade my dreams
And I feel helpless and afraid,
I need to remember your powerful hands
And feel your strong protection.

Emily (aged sixteen)

For a full list of
Dalesman books, calendars,
videos, DVDs, cassettes
and magazines, visit
www.dalesman.co.uk
or telephone
(+44) 01756 701033